Preventing Sexual Assault and Harassment

SEXUAL VIOLENCE AND HARASSMENT

ABUSE AMONG FAMILY AND FRIENDS

COPING WITH SEXUAL VIOLENCE AND HARASSMENT

DEALING WITH DATING AND ROMANCE

PREVENTING SEXUAL ASSAULT AND HARASSMENT

Preventing Sexual Assault and Harassment

H.W. Poole

MASON CREST
PHILADELPHIA · MIAMI

Mason Crest
450 Parkway Drive, Suite D
Broomall, Pennsylvania 19008
(866) MCP-BOOK (toll-free)
www.masoncrest.com

First printing
9 8 7 6 5 4 3 2 1

ISBN (hardback) 978-1-4222-4203-2
ISBN (series) 978-1-4222-4199-8
2ISBN (ebook) 978-1-4222-7609-9
Cataloging-in-Publication Data on file with the Library of Congress.

NATIONAL HIGHLIGHTS

Developed and Produced by National Highlights Inc.
Editor: Peter Jaskowiak
Interior and cover design: Annemarie Redmond
Production: Michelle Luke

QR CODES AND LINKS TO THIRD-PARTY CONTENT
You may gain access to certain third-party content ("Third-Party Sites") by scanning and using the QR Codes that appear in this publication (the "QR Codes"). We do not operate or control in any respect any information, products, or services on such Third-Party Sites linked to by us via the QR Codes included in this publication, and we assume no responsibility for any materials you may access using the QR Codes. Your use of the QR Codes may be subject to terms, limitations, or restrictions set forth in the applicable terms of use or otherwise established by the owners of the Third-Party Sites. Our linking to such Third-Party Sites via the QR Codes does not imply an endorsement or sponsorship of such Third-Party Sites or the information, products, or services

TABLE OF CONTENTS

KEY ICONS TO LOOK FOR:

Words to Understand: These words with their easy-to-understand definitions will increase the reader's understanding of the text, while building vocabulary skills.

Sidebars: This boxed material within the main text allows readers to build knowledge, gain insights, explore possibilities, and broaden their perspectives by weaving together additional information to provide realistic and holistic perspectives.

Educational Videos: Readers can view videos by scanning our QR codes, providing them with additional educational content to supplement the text. Examples include news coverage, moments in history, speeches, iconic sports moments, and much more!

Text-Dependent Questions: These questions send the reader back to the text for more careful attention to the evidence presented there.

Research Projects: Readers are pointed toward areas of further inquiry connected to each chapter. Suggestions are provided for projects that encourage deeper research and analysis.

Series Glossary of Key Terms: This back-of-the-book glossary contains terminology used throughout the series. Words found here increase the reader's ability to read and comprehend higher-level books and articles in this field.

SERIES INTRODUCTION

You may have heard the statistics. One in 4 girls and 1 in 6 boys are sexually abused before turning 18 years old. About 20 percent of American women are raped at some point in their lives. An online survey in 2018 found that approximately 81 percent of women have experienced some form of harassment.

Crimes like these have been happening for a very long time, but stigma surrounding these issues has largely kept them in the shadows. Recent events such as the Me Too movement, the criminal prosecutions of men like Bill Cosby and Dr. Larry Nassar, and the controversy surrounding the confirmation of Judge Brett Kavanaugh to the U.S. Supreme Court have brought media attention to sexual violence and harassment. As it often happens, increased media attention to a social problem is excellent in many ways – the availability of information can help people avoid being victimized, while also letting survivors know that they are not alone. Unfortunately, the media spotlight sometimes shines more heat than light, leaving us with even more questions than we had when we started.

Teen Dating Violence Hotline

1-866-331-9474

TTY: 1-866-331-8453

En Español: 1–800–799–7233

Text: "loveis" to 22522

That is particularly true for young people, who are just dipping their toes into the proverbial dating pool and taking their first steps into the workplace. Two volumes in this set (*Preventing Sexual Assault and Harassment* and *Coping with Sexual*

Assault and Harassment) address the "before" and "after" of those very difficult situations. The volume *Dealing with Dating* looks at romance – how to date as safely as

National Sexual Assault Hotline
1-800-656-HOPE (4673)
Online chat: https://www.rainn.org

possible, how to build emotionally healthy relationships, and what to do if something goes wrong. And finally, *Abuse among Family and Friends* takes a look at the painful issue of sexual abuse and exploitation of minors – the vast majority of whom are abused not by strangers, but by family members, acquaintances, and authority figures who are already in the young person's life. These books hope to provide a trustworthy, accessible resource for readers who have questions they might hesitate to ask in person. *What is consent really about, anyway? What do I do if I have been assaulted? How do I go on a date and not be scared? Will my past sexual abuse ruin my future relationships?* And much more.

In addition to the text, a key part of these books is the regularly appearing "Fact Check" sidebar. Each of these special features takes on common myths and misconceptions and provides the real story. Meanwhile, "Find Out More" boxes and dynamic video links are scattered throughout the book. They, along with the "Further Reading" pages at the end, encourage readers to reach out beyond the confines of these pages. There are extraordinary counselors, activists, and hotline operators all over North America who are eager to help young people with their questions and concerns. What to do about sexual violence and harassment is a vital but difficult conversation; these books aspire to be the beginning of that discussion, not the end.

INTRODUCTION

Sexual assault. Harassment. Abuse. These are big social problems—so big, in fact, that the idea of preventing them might seem too overwhelming to contemplate. How can we possibly stop such things from happening? This book strives to find some answers.

It's important to be careful with our language when we talk about "preventing" sexual misconduct. Discussions about how to prevent assault, for example, should not be confused with blaming people who've experienced it. Consider the public discourse about the connection between alcohol and sexual assault. Too often, what begins as a (presumably) well-intentioned conversation about how to reduce the rates of assault on college campuses devolves into moralistic posturing about how young women really shouldn't drink so much. It's absolutely true that choosing not to drink at a party is a good risk-reduction strategy—not just for young women, by the way, but for anyone. However, saying that is not the same as saying that a young woman who does opt to drink at a party has somehow invited her own attack.

Here's the truth: we can do everything right, obey every rule, and follow every "risk-management strategy," but it won't change the fact that the modern world is, by definition, a risky business. There is no completely risk-free existence.

Still, knowledge is power. In 2014 a group of researchers released their

study of a sexual assault prevention program called Real Consent. They found that six months after the program was held, rates of sexual assault among participants had dropped by 73 percent compared to a control group. This suggests that greater education about the issue creates an opportunity to make a real difference.

FACT CHECK!

Myth: *If someone doesn't report a sexual assault right away, it probably didn't happen or wasn't all that bad.*

Truth: There are a lot of reasons survivors don't report immediately. They may fear retribution from their attacker, or that they won't be believed. They may feel pressured by others to stay silent, or their own shame may silence them.

Large-scale social problems are, at their base, collections of actions taken by individuals. When viewed this way—as a series of small choices made by large numbers of people—preventing sexual misconduct seems like a more achievable goal. Not every assault can be stopped all at once, but we can make gradual change, one person at a time.

In these pages, you'll find out about the myriad types of sexual misconduct and why they occur. We'll bust some common myths about sex and relationships. You'll also get some guidance about choices that could help reduce your risk of ending up on the receiving end of sexual misconduct. You, your friends, and your community can all be part of the solution and help end sexual assault and harassment.

WORDS TO UNDERSTAND

cisgender: describes a person whose gender identity matches that person's biological sex

consent: agreement or permission

felony: a category of serious crime; felony crimes come in several degrees, with "first degree" being the most serious, "second degree" being slightly less serious, and so on

incapacitated: describes the condition of being unable to respond, move, or understand

LGBTQ: an acronym for lesbian, gay, bisexual, transgender, and queer/questioning

pervasive: describes something that is everywhere

PTSD: an acronym for post-traumatic stress disorder, a serious psychological condition caused by disturbing experiences

simulate: fake or pretend

synonyms: two or more terms that mean the same thing

SEXUAL MISCONDUCT: DEFINITIONS

Sexual misconduct is a catch-all term referring to a variety of behaviors that range from socially unacceptable to outright criminal. Some forms of sexual misconduct are clearly and obviously against the law. Others, though not strictly illegal, are still considered out of bounds by reasonable people. But sometimes it can be a challenge to determine what the boundaries are – in other words, what is "reasonable" to one person may not be "reasonable" to someone else.

In 1964 the U.S. Supreme Court issued a ruling on the subject of pornography. Justice Potter Stewart wrote that while pornography is not always easy to define, "I know it when I see it." Unfortunately, while a lot of sexual misconduct is clear-cut, there are also gray areas that fall into that "know-it-when-I-see-it" category. In this chapter, we'll look at the wide range of behaviors that fall under the "misconduct" umbrella, and we'll grapple with what the various terms precisely mean.

WHAT ARE SEXUAL ASSAULT AND RAPE?

Rape is the act of one person forcing sexual intercourse on another person without **consent**. The term *rape* is also usually understood to mean not only penetration of the body, but also unwilling oral sexual activity. Both women and men can be raped, and both women and men can rape.

The terms *sexual assault* and *rape* are often used as **synonyms** in casual conversation. But when it comes to the law, the terms don't always mean the same thing. Under the law, sexual assault is sometimes understood to mean unwelcome sexual contact that stops short of rape, such as kissing or groping.

Here's the tricky part: there is no single definition of either *rape* or *sexual assault* under U.S. law. That's because the terms are defined by individual states. This can get complicated, because different states have different understandings of what these words mean. For instance, the laws of Pennsylvania define rape as unwanted sexual intercourse involving violence or the threat of violence — the exact term they use is *forcible compulsion*. Meanwhile, the same act,

FACT CHECK!

Myth: *The typical rapist is a stranger waiting in a dark alley for a woman in a short skirt to walk by.*

Fact: Only about one-quarter of rapes are committed by strangers. About three-quarters of the time, the rapist is someone the victim knows.

FIND OUT MORE

The Rape, Abuse, & Incest National Network (RAINN) has a useful website where you can look up the sexual misconduct laws in your state. Point your browser to https://apps.rainn.org/policy.

CRIME AND PUNISHMENT

In the United States, the average sentence for someone convicted of rape is around 10 years. However, convicted rapists only serve an average of about 4 years in jail, because sentences are often reduced for various reasons. According to the advocacy group RAINN, only about 6 out of 1,000 rapists serve *any* time whatsoever.

A rape conviction can trigger the death penalty in a number of countries, including China, Egypt, and Saudi Arabia. A death sentence for rape in the United States was ruled unconstitutional in 1977.

The 2017 protest known as Million Women Rise, in London, England, focused on ending violence against women.

but without the threat, is classified as sexual assault. So, sexual assault is a second-degree **felony** in Pennsylvania, while rape is a first-degree (or more serious) crime. However, what Pennsylvania calls "rape," the state of Texas calls "aggravated sexual assault," and Florida calls "sexual battery."

The bottom line is that sexual intercourse with a person who did not actively consent is rape. That includes situations where the person is too young to legally give consent. A 14-year-old may *think* he or she can give consent, but as far as the law is concerned, that's not true. Usually, this crime is called *statutory* rape. Sexual intercourse with someone who is unconscious or otherwise **incapacitated** also falls under the category of rape or sexual assault. Again, different states have different standards for who is able to give consent under what circumstances.

WHAT IS SEXUAL ABUSE?

Sometimes the term *sexual abuse* is used as a synonym for sexual assault, or as a catch-all term for any type of harmful behavior related to sex. But the last thing we need is another generic term, so in this book we'll use *sexual abuse* in its most narrow meaning: when someone in a position of power takes sexual advantage of a person with less power. A doctor who takes sexual advantage of a patient is one example – the doctor is in a more powerful position than the patient.

The most troubling type of sexual abuse by far involves children. Any form of sexual activity with a child is abusive. This includes not only intercourse and sexual touching, but also taking explicit photos of the child or showing the child explicit photos. So-called dirty talk with a child is also sexual abuse.

There is no grey area when it comes to this particular crime. It doesn't matter if the child "seems mature." It doesn't matter if the sexual behavior is real or **simulated**. It doesn't matter if the activity occurs in person or on the Internet. It also doesn't matter if the activity was forced or if the child was somehow "talked into" participating. Children are not capable of

Relationship of Child Abuse Victim to Perpetrator

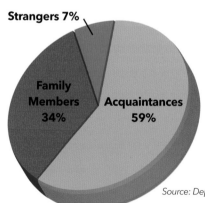

Strangers 7%

Family Members 34%

Acquaintances 59%

The vast majority of child sexual abuse is perpetrated by someone the child knows, including family members, neighbors, parents' friends, teachers, babysitters, and so on. According to the U.S. Department of Justice, strangers make up only 7 percent of all child sexual abuse cases.

Source: Department of Justice, Office of Justice Programs, Bureau of Justice Statistics.

WHO IS A CHILD?

The term *age of consent* refers to laws that determine when someone is considered old enough to give legal consent for sexual activity. In the United States, age of consent is determined by individual states, and it ranges from 16 to 18. Canada's age of consent is 16 across the entire country. Consent laws in Mexico are extremely complex and can vary from age 18 all the way down to 12 in certain contexts.

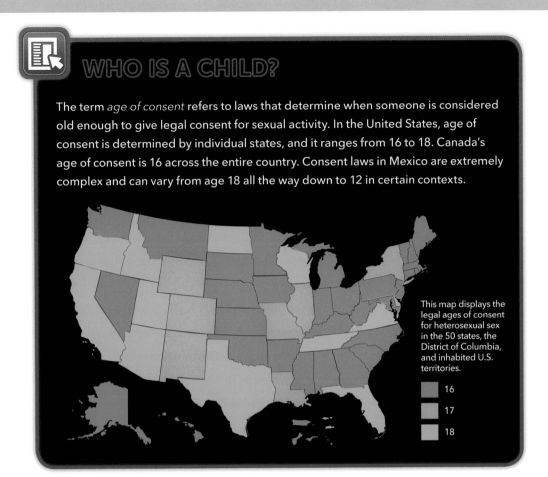

This map displays the legal ages of consent for heterosexual sex in the 50 states, the District of Columbia, and inhabited U.S. territories.

▪ 16
▪ 17
▪ 18

understanding what they're agreeing to, and consequently they cannot give consent to sexual activity, even if they think they can.

One reason sexual abuse is taken so seriously is because of the extremely damaging effects it has on the kids themselves. Surviving sexual abuse can leave kids with severe depression, anxiety, eating disorders, **PTSD**, and many other problems. Other research suggests that children who survive sexual abuse are more likely to engage in high-risk behaviors as adults, which can lead to sexually transmitted diseases (STDs), unplanned pregnancies, and being victimized again by further sexual violence. The American Counseling Association reported a 42 percent increase in suicidal thoughts in kids who survived sexual abuse.

WHAT IS SEXUAL HARASSMENT?

Sexual harassment is a broad category of misconduct that occurs in the workplace. Offensive sexual remarks, demands for sexual favors, and unwanted physical contact are just a few examples of actions that could be sexual harassment. Other examples include displaying pornographic imagery in the workplace; intrusive, sexually explicit questions or remarks; and leering, name-calling, or taunts of a sexual nature. The key point is that the person who is the "focus" of the harassment is expected to put up with the behavior as a condition of keeping his or her job.

Importantly, interactions between teachers and students are also covered under sexual harassment law. That's because a school or university is, in effect, the "workplace" of not only the teachers, but the students as well.

Corporations can be held accountable for the misconduct of their employees. For example, in 2013 a group of employees at a Red Lobster

The term *workplace* doesn't only refer to offices and factory floors. It's understood to include educational settings like classrooms, too.

restaurant in Salisbury, Maryland, filed a hostile work environment complaint against the company. A supervisor had been engaging in groping and other nonconsensual sexual behaviors, and when the workers complained, the restaurant failed to do anything to fix the situation. Red Lobster eventually paid about $160,000 in damages to the people who were harassed.

FACT CHECK!

Myth: *For behavior to qualify as sexual harassment, it has to come from a boss, teacher, or someone "higher up" than you.*

Fact: A person's level of authority is not a factor in sexual harassment cases. While it is common for these behaviors to come from higher up, harassment by coworkers, fellow students, or customers is still harassment.

Under federal U.S. law, sexual harassment is a type of gender discrimination, and it's forbidden by Title VII of the Civil Rights Act of 1964. The law applies to all companies with 15 or more employees, and it recognizes two broad types of sexual harassment: quid pro quo and hostile work environment. (In schools, sexual harassment is covered under Title IX of the Educational Amendments Act of 1972; find out more about this on page 55.)

WHAT IS QUID PRO QUO?

The term *quid pro quo* is a Latin phrase that means "something for something." For instance, if an employer demands sexual activity in exchange for a promotion, that's quid pro quo sexual harassment. If a boss tells an employee that she must date him or she'll get fired, that also is quid pro quo harassment. Keep in mind, though, that the threat doesn't need to be quite that blatant; an implied quid pro quo, while harder to prove, is still harassment.

What's more, prospective employers can also be guilty of quid pro quo harassment. For instance, the actresses Ashley Judd and Mira Sorvino alleged that after they rejected sexual advances from the movie mogul Harvey Weinstein, he took deliberate steps to damage their careers. If the allegations are true, that's evidence of quid pro quo harassment, because Weinstein used his power to punish the women for refusing his demands.

WHAT IS A HOSTILE WORK ENVIRONMENT?

The second type of harassment, *hostile work environment*, involves activities like sharing explicit images, making sexually inappropriate remarks, and unwelcome physical contact. These behaviors interfere with the victim's ability to do his or her job. Legally, these behaviors need to be repeated and **pervasive**.

The concepts of *repeated* and *pervasive* are very important here. If a person acts like a jerk one time, that's bad, but it's not necessarily harassment. Someone telling a dirty joke at work does not in itself create a hostile work environment. But if the jokes continue, or if they are accompanied by, let's say, the forwarding of nude photographs on office e-mail or repeated unwelcome physical contact, that's starting to sound a lot like a hostile work environment. And if employees complain about the problem to a supervisor, and the supervisor does not take any action to fix it, then you are definitely looking at a sexual harassment problem.

This video talks about sexual harassment in the workplace.

WHAT IS INTIMATE PARTNER VIOLENCE?

Intimate partner violence (IPV) refers to assaults between two people who are (or used to be) romantically involved. Sometimes you may hear other terms used for this crime, including spousal battery, spousal assault or rape, domestic violence, relationship violence, dating abuse, or dating violence. All these terms refer to the same thing.

The reality is that sexual abuse in an intimate relationship doesn't happen in a vacuum; it often comes hand-in-hand with other types of abuse, such as physical and emotional abuse. That's why IPV is understood to include a wide range of damaging behaviors, some sexual and some not.

IS IPV DIFFERENT FROM RAPE?

Sexual assault is always illegal, regardless of the relationship between the perpetrator and victim. Given that, you might wonder why IPV is discussed as a separate category. If "rape is rape," then why do we even treat some cases differently from others?

In the strictest sense, there is no difference between assault by a stranger and assault by someone you know – either way, the person was still assaulted. However, courts generally view a physical assault by a romantic partner as being fundamentally different from an assault by a stranger, and as a result the punishments are often different. And while rape is *always* illegal, some states do have slightly different laws when it comes to IPV. For example, some states have stricter rules on how long you can wait before reporting sexual abuse by a partner as opposed to an acquaintance or stranger.

But the finer points of law aren't the only reason why IPV is different from other types of sexual assault. In the messy world of real life, there are a lot of

FACT CHECK!

Myth: *A husband cannot technically rape his wife because of the preexisting legal relationship between them.*

Fact: Forcing sexual activity on someone without consent is *always* a crime. Wedding vows do not erase a person's rights to consent or not consent.

complex issues that arise with IPV that may not be present in other situations. People in intimate relationships have feelings for one another – that fact alone can make IPV harder to understand, harder to report, and harder to stop. There are also larger contextual factors. People in intimate relationships may share a home, they may be raising children, and one person may depend on the other for financial support. These external factors can make it much harder for people to leave abusive relationships, even though they want to.

It is a horrifying fact that women are more likely to be killed by someone they love than by a stranger. The Centers for Disease Control and Prevention (CDC) analyzed more than 10,000 homicides between the years 2003 and 2014 and found that 55 percent of female homicide victims died at the hands of a current or former intimate partner.

DOES IPV ONLY HAPPEN TO STRAIGHT, MARRIED PEOPLE?

The stereotype of an IPV survivor usually involves an adult woman being abused by her husband. That's unfortunately common, but it's not the whole story. IPV can be an issue for any two people who are romantically involved, regardless of age, gender, or marital status.

Teens can and do experience abuse in their relationships. In fact, as many as one in three teenagers has experienced some form of abuse from someone he or she was dating. That abuse can come in various forms, including physical, verbal, sexual, or digital (online). Sometimes people assume that if you are "just dating" then the abuse "doesn't count." But this isn't true. It is not normal or okay for *anyone* to hit you, stalk you, humiliate you, try to control your actions, or pressure you into sexual activity.

Even if you aren't having sex with the person you're dating – even if you've never had sex with *anyone* – that doesn't make your relationship immune. That's why some experts prefer the term *dating abuse* rather than *intimate partner violence*. It's a way to remind you that even if you aren't yet "intimate" with someone, it doesn't mean that abuse somehow doesn't matter.

People in **LGBTQ** relationships also experience IPV. In fact, it's been estimated that abuse occurs at the same rate, or even higher rates, among LGBTQ people as it does among those who are straight and **cisgender**. Abuse in intimate relationships has nothing to do with the age or sexual orientation of the people involved; it has to do with abuse of power. IPV can affect anyone, regardless of age, sexuality, gender identification, or marital status.

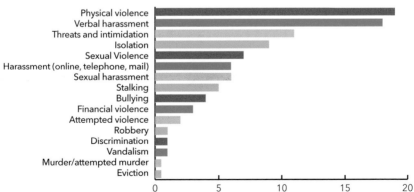

Types of IPV Reported in the LGBTQ Community

In 2016 the National Coalition of Anti-Violence Programs surveyed more than 2,000 survivors of IPV in the LGBTQ and HIV-positive communities. The survey asked what type of abuse occurred. (Respondents were allowed to choose more than one type.) It's worth noting that these complaints include the same types of incidents that occur in straight relationships.

Source: National Coalition of Antiviolence Programs, http://avp.org/wp-content/uploads/2017/11/NCAVP-IPV-Report-2016.pdf.

WHAT IS STALKING?

Another type of sexual misconduct is called *stalking*. Stalking is when someone repeatedly acts in ways that are designed to make another person feel intimidated or threatened. Stalkers often spy on their victims, contact them constantly, track their activities (in real life and/or online), and send messages with implied or explicit threats.

Although men and women can both stalk and be stalked, men are more frequently the stalkers and women are more often the targets. For instance, it's not uncommon for women who flee IPV to be stalked by their exes. But stalking can also occur within committed relationships. And other times, the intimate relationship only exists in the mind of the stalker.

Not all stalking qualifies as sexual misconduct. Someone may stalk another person for any number of reasons. You've probably heard of "celebrity stalkers," for instance – people who become obsessed with a particular celebrity, to the point where they may break into their homes or even try to hurt them.

Regardless of the context, authorities take stalking seriously because of how quickly it can escalate from words to actions. It's not uncommon for stalkers to take part in increasingly aggressive activities like vandalism, breaking and entering, and even assault.

FIND OUT MORE

If you suspect that you're being stalked, you should try to keep a record (or "log") of every time your stalker attempts to contact you. This type of documentation may be enormously helpful down the road, especially if you need to get authorities involved. The National Center for Victims of Crime provides a sample log on its website, at http://victimsofcrime. org/docs/src/stalking-incident-log_pdf.

IS THERE A CONNECTION BETWEEN HARASSMENT AND THE INTERNET?

Thanks to modern technology, we have more ways of contacting one another than ever before, including cell phones, e-mail, and a variety of social media applications. Unfortunately, all these points of contact can make harassment easier to engage in. What's more, some devices and apps make our *real-world* locations easier to track, which presents a huge problem for people who are being stalked. The legal term for using the Internet to track, harass, and threaten someone else is *cyberstalking*.

The Internet has also opened up opportunities for new and terrible types of harassment. For example, *revenge porn* refers to the act of posting images and videos of people in intimate situations without the permission of the people involved. As the name suggests, revenge porn is usually related to an ex who gets angry about being rejected and decides to "expose" and humiliate the victim. Sometimes there is a blackmail aspect to revenge porn, too — as in, "pay me or I will release this embarrassing material."

Then there's *doxing,* which is the term for finding and posting someone's private contact information. Doxing invites others to contact, harass, and even stalk victims in their real lives. Some doxing cases have a gender component — such as when women were doxed during an online controversy called GamerGate. Many other cases have nothing to do with gender, but that doesn't make doxing any less harmful.

The term *cyberbullying* refers to all manner of different ways people extend meanness to cyberspace and make one another miserable online. According to the Cyberbullying Research Center, around 28 percent of students say they have experienced cyberbullying at some point.

WHAT ARE HATE CRIMES?

A *hate crime* is a crime that is partly or entirely motivated by a feeling of hatred toward a particular group of people. Murder, rape, assault, and vandalism can all be hate crimes, depending the motivation of the perpetrator.

It's important to understand that being hateful isn't itself against the law. The First Amendment to the U.S. Constitution forbids the government from making it illegal to hold any opinion, no matter how terrible others may think that opinion is. But the First Amendment only protects speech and thought – it does not protect *actions*. Hate crimes are actions that are deliberately taken to hurt or intimidate others, specifically because of their membership in a particular group. Hate crime legislation does not create "new" crimes; instead, it puts an additional penalty on behavior that was already criminal.

Hate crime laws grew out of the civil rights movement of the 1960s, and consequently they were originally focused on racially motivated crimes. Over time, other minority groups have been added to the list of "protected classes." For our purposes in this book, the most important additions are gender, gender identity (for instance, being transgender), and sexual orientation. Federal laws covering hate crimes against women and the LGBTQ community include the Violent Crime Control and Law Enforcement Act (1994) and the Matthew Shepard and James Byrd, Jr., Hate Crimes Prevention Act (2009). In addition to these federal statutes, more than half of U.S. states have additional hate crime laws that also protect some or all of these groups.

FIND OUT MORE

The Human Rights Campaign (HRC) keeps track of laws protecting the LGBTQ community from discrimination and hate crimes. You can find out more about laws in your state here: http://www.hrc.org/state-maps.

The FBI is responsible for tallying hate crimes and reporting the data; in 2017 they reported 6,100 confirmed hate crimes in the previous year. That said, statistics on hate crimes can be hard to come by, especially when it comes to the LGBTQ community. Victims are sometimes reluctant to come forward, for a variety of reasons. Some may fear being "outed" as LGBTQ, while others fear being dismissed or further discriminated against by authorities.

TEXT-DEPENDENT QUESTIONS

1. Why is there such variation in definitions of sexual assault?
2. When it comes to abuse, who presents the greatest threat to children: people they know or people they don't?
3. What types of behaviors can contribute to a hostile work environment?
4. What are some other terms that people sometimes use with regard to IPV?
5. What is doxing?

RESEARCH PROJECT

Find out about laws regarding sexual misconduct in your own state, then choose a second state that interests you. Compare and contrast the laws – how are they alike, and how are they different? You can begin your research at the RAINN website referenced earlier (https://apps.rainn.org/policy), or look up the text of sexual misconduct legislation at state websites or your library.

WORDS TO UNDERSTAND

agency: the ability to act on one's own

discrepancy: when two things that should line up in some way don't match

inherent: built in, essential

nebulous: vague, not well defined

norms: standards of what's considered typical or "normal" for a particular group or situation

promiscuous: describes someone with many short-term sexual partners

psychosis: mental impairment so severe the person loses connection with reality

self-esteem: a person's sense of his or her own value

2

THE ROOTS OF SEXUAL MISCONDUCT

Before we can talk about how we — as a society, as communities, and as individuals — can prevent sexual misconduct, it's important to understand why it occurs. However, any discussion about root causes needs to be prefaced by a couple of ideas.

First, no two situations are exactly alike. There is a human tendency to generalize — to say that men are like this and women are like that, or that men *always* do X and women *always* do Y. Such assumptions are rarely correct. They can be useful to identify particular trends, of course. But just because we notice that something *often* happens, that doesn't mean it *always* happens, or that the same explanation applies every time.

Second, the theories discussed here are just that: theories. This chapter intends to introduce you to some of the most important ongoing discussions as our society struggles to deal with the issue of sexual misconduct. Not every analyst or expert agrees with every theory.

Last but not least: to try and understand why a certain event took place is *not* to say the event is acceptable. To understand something better is not to condone it. The potential causes discussed in this chapter are not excuses.

PSYCHOLOGY AND SEXUAL MISCONDUCT

Who commits sexual misconduct? The only perfect answer to this question is, "potentially, anyone." There is no single type or profile of a rapist or sexual harasser. But although we can't say there's a specific "type" of person who commits sexual misconduct, decades of research have given us a basic understanding of certain psychological factors that can play a role in those behaviors.

PEER PRESSURE

The sociologist Walter DeKeseredy, who is director of West Virginia University's Research Center on Violence, argues that young men in particular are highly vulnerable to peer pressure when it comes to sexual misconduct.

DeKeseredy argues that young men are less motivated by sexual desire than they are by a sense that they need to "prove" something to their peer group. Consequently, peer groups that accept or even encourage these kinds of behaviors are likely to inspire more of them.

A NOTE ON GENDER

As discussed here, perpetrators of sexual assault are overwhelmingly male. Furthermore, their victims are overwhelmingly female. According to statistics from the U.S. Bureau of Justice, 90 percent of sexual assault survivors are female. That's why you so often see perpetrators referred to as male and victims and survivors as female. Discussions often focus on that dynamic because it's so common.

But it's important to note that the genders don't always break down in such a simple way. Men can also be victims of sexual assault – statistically, it's usually committed by other men, but women can also commit sexual assault.

DEMOGRAPHICS

We don't know nearly as much as we should about who commits sexual misconduct and why. The National Crime Victimization Survey found that only 23 percent of sexual assaults were reported to police. (The same survey found that 80 percent of car thefts were reported.) When only 23 percent of the crimes are ever reported at all, and fewer than that are investigated, we aren't left with a good foundation of data.

From the limited data we do have, we know that between 90 and 95 percent of perpetrators are male. They are also more likely to be Caucasian: 57 percent of perpetrators are white, 27 percent are black, and the remainder are some other race or of mixed race.

As DeKeseredy told a reporter, "What we find with college students is that those who are most likely to sexually assault women have friends who encourage that and friends who do it. . . . If men in these groups feel that they're not getting as much sex as their friends, then they're more likely to engage in sexual aggression so that they could live up to their peers' expectations."

SELF-ESTEEM

Another psychological factor appears to be **self-esteem**. To have self-esteem means that you believe you are worthy of kindness and respect. Healthy self-esteem is a bit like "Goldilocks and the Three Bears" – the ideal amount lies somewhere between too little and too much.

Psychologists have theorized that some people who commit sexual assault have too much self-esteem. This excessive confidence (or "entitlement") leads them to believe their desires are more important than everyone else's. If someone believes that other people fundamentally have less value, then that person may tell himself that he has the right to do whatever he likes to them.

According to statistics from the U.S. Department of Justice, women aged 18 to 24 who are not in college are three times more likely to experience sexual violence than women who are older. Meanwhile, women in the same age group who are in college are *four* times more likely to experience sexual violence.

On the other hand, some people who commit sexual assault seem to have *low* self-esteem. They fear they'll never earn the respect of others because, deep down, they don't believe they deserve it. This can build into an overwhelming sense of frustration, causing the person to lash out in the form of sexual assault. Poor self-esteem also makes people more easily led by others and overly eager to please them.

ANGER

Anger is sometimes a psychological component of sexual assault, especially a type of anger called *vindictiveness*. To be vindictive means that you are not only angry, but also that you desire to hurt the people who (you believe) wronged you. Some sexual assaults are vindictive in a direct way. For example, a physically abusive husband might also sexually abuse his wife as part of a larger expression of his rage.

Other times, vindictiveness is spread across an entire group. Some men who have sexually assaulted women express a **nebulous** vindictiveness at the entire female gender. Another word for this is *misogyny*, or the hatred of women. By assaulting one person, their generalized anger gains a specific target, who becomes an imaginary "stand in" for women in general.

LACK OF EMPATHY

Another common trait among people who commit sexual misconduct is a lack of empathy. Empathy is the ability to understand what another person might be going through. At its root, empathy is an imaginative act: it forces you to consider what it *might feel like* to be in a particular situation.

It's easy to see how a lack of empathy can play into sexual misconduct. Clearly, being on the receiving end of sexual misconduct feels extremely bad, and an empathic person is inclined to avoid behaviors that make other people feel terrible. But if you lack the ability to feel empathy for other people, then that's one less thing to stop you from behaving however you want.

MENTAL ILLNESS

One more psychological component, which is rare but can't be ignored completely, is mental illness. A minority of people who commit sexual assault are experiencing a type of **psychosis**. But it's important to be very clear that the number of rapists who exhibit genuine mentally illness is extremely small. The idea of a disease called *coercive paraphilia* – put simply, "getting off" on rape – has long been a subject of controversy. So far, every time the discussion is raised, psychologists reach the same conclusion: rape is consistently affirmed as a criminal question (requiring jail time) and not a mental illness question (requiring treatment).

> "Different sexual offenders have deficits in different domains. Many rapists, for example, fully understand the harm they are inflicting on their victims, but this does not stop them because they have hostile intentions. Other offenders truly fail to appreciate the harm they caused. Still other sexual offenders know their offenses are hurtful, but are too ashamed to admit it."
>
> –R. K. Hanson, "Empathy Deficits of Sexual Offenders," *Journal of Sexual Aggression*

THE ROLE OF GENDER NORMS

Even in the 21st century, we all understand that there are certain traditional notions about how genders are "supposed to" think and act. These ideas aren't biologically determined — that is, male and female brains are fundamentally the same. And yet men are expected to be more aggressive and dominant, while women are expected to be more emotional and passive. These are "gender **norms**." Some people reject these norms, while others embrace them. But whatever we think of them, we all know what they are. Studies suggest that even young children pick up on gender norms very early in life.

Over the past decades, gender norms for women have become considerably more flexible than they used to be. Most people no longer find it strange to see a woman as a boss or a leader, for example. But gender norms for men haven't always kept up with the evolution of norms for women. That is, while it is increasingly more acceptable for women to take dominant positions, it's still often considered unacceptable for men to take on more feminine norms. Doing so can result in something sociologists call *gender-discrepancy stress*.

For example, let's say a boy gets hurt on the soccer field, and he cries because he's in pain. His friends mock him for crying, and the coach tells him to "man up." This can leave the boy not only physically injured,

Check out this video from the U.S. military about assault prevention.

Despite all the evolution in our ideas about gender norms, we still tend to believe that men who show "too much" vulnerability are somehow weak or unmasculine.

but also psychologically wounded, because he is perceived as not being "tough enough." Gender-discrepancy stress is the worry some men have that if they don't act in a certain way, they will lose their "man card" and no longer be perceived as truly masculine.

Gender-discrepancy stress is suspected to be a factor in some sexual misconduct. A 2015 study in the *Journal of Adolescent Health* found that boys who reported gender-discrepancy stress were more likely to "act out" in aggressive ways. According to the study, "boys who experience stress about being perceived as 'sub-masculine' may be more likely to engage in sexual violence as a means of demonstrating their masculinity to self and/or others."

WHAT IS TOXIC MASCULINITY?

The term *toxic masculinity* gets tossed around a lot in today's pop culture, but it can be a bit tricky to figure out what it actually means. The most important thing to understand is that the term does not mean that there is something bad about being male. If you've heard the term used that way, it was used incorrectly.

When used accurately, toxic masculinity refers to a *specific type* of gender norm, not the gender itself. Specifically, toxic masculinity refers to the gender norm that suggests you have to be tough, unemotional, and aggressive to qualify as a "a real man."

Think of toxic masculinity as more than just a term: think of it as an entire argument. The argument being made is that when traits like empathy and kindness are considered incompatible with being a "real man," it's poisonous, or toxic, to everyone involved — not just women, but men, too.

WHAT IS OBJECTIFICATION?

Objectification is viewing a fellow human being as an object that can be owned, used, and discarded. Objectifying someone denies that person's **agency** – it's like treating someone as a doll that does whatever you want because it has no will of its own.

 Sexual objectification refers to treating another person as though he or she only exists for the purpose of sexual pleasure. "Pleasure" in this context doesn't necessarily mean having intercourse – it can mean that, certainly, but it can also mean simply the pleasure of looking at a "beautiful thing." Advertising is packed with images that feature the human body being used as simply a pile of flesh that's pleasing to the eye.

Objectification describes the practice of looking at a beautiful car and a beautiful woman as though the car and the woman were the same, rather than viewing the woman as a full human being.

LOVE OR MONEY?

The author David Foster Wallace wrote that pornography is "given to us by people who do not love us but want our money." As pornography becomes easier and easier to find, many people worry that teenagers will grow up thinking that "porn sex" is the same as "good sex." The truth is, pornography has about as much to do with real-life sex as, say, a TV show about doctors has to do with what a doctor really does: a little, but not much!

Pornography is also a venue that's overflowing with sexual objectification; it's not unreasonable to say that objectification is what pornography is for. A lot of pornography shows an aggressive version of sexuality, with male dominance as the central theme.

It's clear that sexual objectification can play a role in sexual assault. If the person being assaulted is "not really a person," then there is no need to consider his or her feelings. Some critics have concluded that pornography encourages sexual assault, because it portrays a hypersexualized universe in which the only goal is short-term satisfaction, usually of the male. However, others argue that there is nothing wrong with the fantasy world of pornography; in fact, they say that porn provides an imaginative outlet for people who aren't as sexually active in real life as they wish to be.

But the line between real sexuality and fake, porn-based sexuality can get blurry fast. That's particularly true for younger people, who often have no real-life experience and only know what they've seen on the Internet. As one 14-year-old girl told a reporter for *The Guardian*, "Pornography puts a lot of pressure on girls. A boy will see it and think this woman is gonna do this." She's not wrong: porn has been proven to have a direct impact on what people think bodies are supposed to look like and on which specific sexual activities people are supposed to engage in.

SOCIAL SCRIPTS

In movies and theater, the script is a document that outlines what is supposed to happen. If one actor delivers the line, "I love you," he knows that his scene partner is going to say, "I love you, too," because it's written in the script. The script lets all the performers know what to do and what to expect.

In sociology, a *social script* is the term for patterns of behavior that are widely understood and expected. If you walk into a Starbucks, it's understood that you'll stand in a line to place your order, and then move to another part of the counter to wait for your coffee. Behaviors like standing in line and waiting for one's order are parts of a "how to behave in a coffee shop" script that we've all learned.

Interactions between men and women are also governed by social scripts to a certain extent. One very basic script is that a romantic date progresses from some neutral activity (dinner, a movie, etc.) to physical intimacy. It seems to most of us like that's how dates are "supposed to go." We may have been on dates like that ourselves, or we may have heard about dates that progressed that way; if nothing else, we've seen it happen in films and on TV. There's nothing **inherent** in dating that means dinner *has to* be followed by sexual activity. That's just a widely understood script.

Do you see how the man in this image is in the active position, presenting gifts to the woman, who is lying down in a passive position? That's by design. Even in the 21st century, the social script says it's the man's job to pursue a woman, and her job to be pursued. (The reverse happens all the time, of course! But the *traditional* social script puts the male in the pursuing role.)

SOCIAL SCRIPTS AND YOU

Social scripts can lead to a lot of unexamined expectations. Young men sometimes feel that it's their role to push for as much sex as they can get. After all, sexual aggression is part of our social script about "how men are." The traditional social script also suggests that men value sex over relationships, that they want a lot of partners, and so on. Consequently, a young man who wants to be "a player" may try to meet those expectations, mindlessly following a sexual script that was written long before he existed.

Young women are also influenced by social scripts. Since a date is understood to be "an activity followed by intimacy," a woman may feel obligated to follow through with the intimacy part, even if she doesn't want to. Meanwhile, there is a social expectation that it's the female's job to regulate the sexual behavior of the male. According to the script, "males will try to get sex from you because that's how they are, and it's your job to somehow control their impulses."

If you're thinking, "Wait, doesn't the first female script ('giving in') run counter to the second one ('regulating male impulses')" – the answer is yes. Yes, it does.

Social scripts are extremely tricky! In one sense, they're very useful; they create a shared understanding of "how things should go," and that helps reduce uncertainty and anxiety. But at the same time, traditional social scripts can conflict with individual preferences – not all people want to behave the way their gender is "supposed to" behave. And not only that, social scripts can come into conflict with other scripts, as we just saw.

Can these patterns be broken? Can we "go off script"? Of course! Scripts can be, and are, rewritten all the time. It's not always easy to do, however – social scripts are so programmed into us that we don't always see them. An important component of reducing incidents of sexual misconduct involves helping people to first understand, and then rewrite, some of the social scripts they've grown up with.

SOCIAL SCRIPTS AND SAME-SEX RELATIONSHIPS

Because their relationships are less traditional, people in same-sex relationships inevitably rewrite many social scripts. They can't rely on gendered ideas of who initiates sexual activity, for example. They can't assume which member of the relationship is "supposed to" be emotional, or even who is "supposed to" take out the trash.

That said, LGBTQ people still live in the world, and they are influenced by traditional ideas about gender, just like straight people are. For instance, there is a negative stereotype that suggests gay men are promiscuous. That cliché has roots in the same social script that straight men grow up with — that men are sexually aggressive by nature and are supposed to have as many partners as they can get. That may be true for some, but it isn't true for everyone.

THE ROLE OF ALCOHOL

Alcohol is a socially acceptable drug in many communities. According to the National Survey on Drug Use and Health, slightly over half of Americans aged 12 and up reported drinking alcohol regularly. For many people, alcohol use is strongly associated with social occasions. It lowers inhibitions and can make users feel good for a short while.

Unfortunately, alcohol consumption is associated with a wide variety of serious problems. Health problems caused by excessive alcohol are outside the scope of this book, but they are real and need to be taken seriously. Behavioral problems are in some ways even more worrying. Every year on college campuses, where excessive drinking is rampant, nearly 700,000 physical assaults and 100,000 sexual assaults have some association with alcohol consumption. About 50 percent of sexual assaults on college campuses involve alcohol use.

It would oversimplify matters to say alcohol "caused" these assaults in any direct way. At the same time, it would be naive to pretend that alcohol plays no role. Sexual misconduct frequently happens in settings that also involve drinking, like parties. In fact, some perpetrators seek out these settings specifically to find vulnerable targets.

Drinking can play a role in sexual assault in other ways, too. In particular, alcohol causes the following symptoms:

- impaired judgement
- increased aggression
- loss of ability to resist assault
- harmful assumptions about the "availability" of females who drink

After the fact, alcohol is sometimes used as an excuse for misconduct, shifting responsibility from the perpetrator to the victim. A double standard comes into play: a young man drinks because that's what young men do, but a young woman who drinks has "brought it on herself." As a result, people who are assaulted while drinking experience higher levels of self-blame, and they are even less likely to report the assault. Particularly if the survivor is an underage drinker, she may be afraid to report what happened for fear of "getting in trouble" or upsetting her parents or other adults. Sexual predators know this to be true. Some use alcohol deliberately, not only to "loosen up" their prey, but also to help insulate themselves from future consequences.

FACT CHECK!

Myth: *It's safer to drink beer instead of "hard" liquor like vodka.*

Fact: Alcohol is alcohol is alcohol. It's all the same stuff, regardless of what form it comes in. A bottle of beer has the same amount of alcohol as a shot of vodka or whiskey, which has the same as a glass of wine.

WHAT ABOUT SEXUAL HARASSMENT?

It's often pointed out that sexual assault is less about sex than it is about power and domination. But sometimes people don't realize that sexual harassment is *also* more about exerting power in the workplace than it is about, say, dating an employee. The root causes of harassment are related to those of sexual assault, but there are some twists.

STAKING OUT TERRITORY

Some people sexually harass coworkers to show dominance over "their territory." Basically, they harass to prove — both to themselves and others — that they can. The behaviors signal to other employees that they are less powerful than the harasser.

Not all harassers are male and not all victims are female, but that is certainly a common scenario. At some level, a man may feel that women "don't belong" in "his" workplace. An endless barrage of dirty jokes and inappropriate touches are his attempts to make sure women know where they stand. Some men are threatened by the idea of women holding positions of power in the workplace. Sexual harassment can be a way of exerting some (inappropriate) control over the situation. It can also be an expression of deep-seated fears or resentments that the perpetrator might not even be consciously aware he feels.

DEMONSTRATING INVINCIBILITY

One reason powerful men sexually harass women is, quite simply, because they can. The very fact that men in positions of authority can behave in ways that would be considered outrageous otherwise is, in itself, part of the appeal.

For the harasser, it's enjoyable to "get away with it." What's more, the act of getting away with it reinforces — *and demonstrates to other men* — that the harasser is every bit as powerful as he thinks he is.

A PERK OF THE JOB

In some fields, successful men have been trained to expect that access to women is part of what they "win" by becoming successful. Hollywood, to take one example, has a long and ugly history of what's called the "casting couch," which is a reference to the idea that actresses get good roles by submitting to the sexual desires of male producers and directors. In the past, men at the

Film producer Harvey Weinstein was accused of sexual harassment or assault by more than 80 women.

"The sexual harassment of women can occur largely because women occupy inferior job positions and job roles; at the same time, sexual harassment works to keep women in such positions. Sexual harassment, then, uses and helps create women's structurally inferior status."

—Catharine MacKinnon, *Sexual Harassment of Working Women* (1979)

top of many different fields have assumed that they are *owed* sexual attention, simply by virtue of their professional accomplishments.

OLD-FASHIONED ATTITUDES

Some men may still refuse to understand why there is a difference between complimenting the work a woman is doing and complimenting the dress she's wearing. Observing that a man may be clueless rather than malicious does *not*

A healthy working environment is one where everyone is treated with respect, regardless of gender.

make his behavior okay, however. Instead, it points to the need for workplace training, to make sure old-timers in the office understand that the world around them has changed.

TEXT-DEPENDENT QUESTIONS

1. What is gender-discrepancy stress?
2. Why might objectification may play a role in sexual misconduct?
3. What percentage of assaults on college campuses involve drinking?
4. Name several ways alcohol can play a role in sexual misconduct.
5. What are some of the reasons people sexually harass others in the workplace?

RESEARCH PROJECT

Watch a film that interests you – it could be any type, from any period. As you watch, keep a list of social scripts and gender norms that you notice. Here are some questions to consider: Which characters make choices and act on them? Which ones are acted upon? How do the men act and speak versus how the women act and speak? Do the characters ever violate what you'd consider to be "traditional" norms? What's the impact of that?

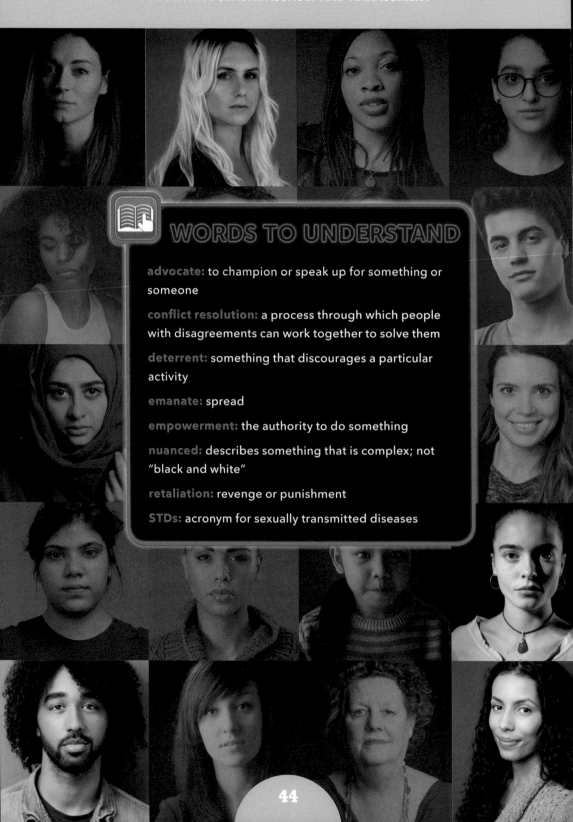

WORDS TO UNDERSTAND

advocate: to champion or speak up for something or someone

conflict resolution: a process through which people with disagreements can work together to solve them

deterrent: something that discourages a particular activity

emanate: spread

empowerment: the authority to do something

nuanced: describes something that is complex; not "black and white"

retaliation: revenge or punishment

STDs: acronym for sexually transmitted diseases

3

PREVENTION: OVERVIEW

People have been trying to figure out how to end sexual violence and harassment for a long time. But the past decade or so has seen a real evolution in how we approach the issue.

In the past — and still, somewhat, today — prevention efforts focused on teaching potential victims to avoid being assaulted or harassed. For example, one often-repeated maxim is that young women at parties should never leave their drinks unattended. And that's good advice: it's far too easy for a would-be predator to slip a drug into an unattended drink. There is nothing wrong with providing tips to help people look after their own safety.

But while a discussion about prevention might begin with personal choices, it's important that it not end there. These days, prevention no longer focuses solely on safety tips. Rather than only teaching potential victims how *not* to get attacked or harassed, the new focus is on teaching potential perpetrators not to do it in the first place. What can we do in our families, communities, and workplaces to make sexual violence and harassment less likely to occur? All of us — old and young, male and female, straight and gay — can help end sexual violence and harassment.

SEXUAL VIOLENCE AND PUBLIC HEALTH

Despite its name, the Centers for Disease Control and Prevention (CDC) is not only interested in literal diseases. The CDC views sexual violence as a public health problem, and the organization has devoted time and energy to studying the issue. In its work, the CDC employs what's called a *social-ecological model*; it's a complicated-sounding term, but all it really means is that none of us live in a vacuum. The decisions we make — good and bad — are strongly influenced by our relationships and our understanding of the world around us. In recognition of this, sexual violence prevention strategies consider four levels: individual, relationship, community, and societal.

INDIVIDUALS

At the individual level, prevention strategies involve learning and practicing new skills, such as communication and **conflict resolution**. Improved interpersonal skills help people figure out ways to deal with conflict that don't involve causing harm. Counseling and therapy can also be useful because they help people learn to interact more productively with others.

Some reduction strategies are gender-specific. For instance, the Coaching Boys into Men program trains athletic coaches on how to encourage forms of masculinity that are less focused on aggression and domination. Meanwhile, young women can benefit from so-called **empowerment**-based training programs, which teach them how to assess risk and better **advocate** for themselves. In Canada, an empowerment program for college freshwomen found a 50 percent reduction in victimization 1 year after the young women attended the program.

SAFE DATES

The goals of this program are . . .

- To raise student awareness of what constitutes healthy and abusive dating relationships.
- To raise student awareness of dating abuse and its causes and consequences.
- To equip students with the skills and resources to help themselves or friends in abusive dating relationships.
- To equip students with the skills to develop healthy dating relationships, including positive communication, anger management, and conflict resolution.

–Safe Dates: Goals, Hazelden Publishing,
https://www.hazelden.org/web/public/safedatesgoals.page

RELATIONSHIPS

On the relationship level, interventions such as family therapy and parenting training can help prevent future sexual misconduct. There are also specific educational programs focused on intimate relationships (such as the Safe Dates program, from the Hazelden Betty Ford Foundation) that encourage emotional awareness, empathy for partners, and better communication. All these interpersonal skills can help reduce the threat of sexual violence.

According to the CDC, sex education also has a role to play. Sex education is primarily focused on sexual health (for instance, reducing the spread of **STDs** and unintended pregnancies). But the same high-risk behaviors that contribute to the spread of STDs are also implicated in sexual violence, so reducing one helps reduce the other. What's more, sex education helps young people understand that when they have a partner, both partners are sharing risks with each other. This has the secondary effect of encouraging a greater sense of empathy, which can help reduce sexual violence.

COMMUNITY

Communities can be any size – there are small ones, like a classroom or a sports team, or large ones, like an entire school or neighborhood. Depending on the type of community, there are many things that can be done to help prevent sexual violence.

In schools and workplaces, prevention begins by taking the issue seriously. Members of the community need to know that if they come forward, their concerns will be heard and acted upon. Numerous studies of college campuses have shown that the vast majority of incidents go unreported because victims lack confidence that their reports will be investigated. Policies about harassment and violence need to be clear and consistently applied to *all* members of the community, not just some.

FIND OUT MORE

The CDC developed an approach to sexual misconduct reduction called STOP SV (sexual violence). The acronym means:

S Promote **Social Norms** That Protect against Violence

T **Teach** Skills to Prevent Sexual Violence

O Provide **Opportunities** to Empower and Support Girls and Women

P Create **Protective** Environments

SV **Support Victims**/Survivors to Lessen Harms

You can find out more about STOP SV here: https://www.cdc.gov/violenceprevention/pdf/SV-Prevention-Technical-Package.pdf.

Another step is for communities to offer services and support to survivors of sexual misconduct. Helping survivors may sound like a separate issue from prevention – after all, if there is a survivor, that by definition means that something was *not* prevented. However, survivor support actually does help reduce future incidents, for a few reasons.

First, sexual misconduct (particularly assault) has long-term impacts on survivors; improving mental health outcomes will make the community stronger in the future. Second, active survivor support sends a clear signal that sexual violence and harassment are not tolerated in the community. This gives community members confidence that their safety matters. It also sends a message to potential perpetrators that their behavior will have consequences.

SOCIETY

Society-level prevention efforts expand on efforts at the community level; rather than a community-wide policy about harassment, for example, a society-level intervention would involve strengthening anti-harassment laws.

Even more broadly, societal prevention involves changing assumptions and attitudes that condone or promote sexual violence. Public education campaigns can also – slowly but surely – help change attitudes. More equal gender norms can be encouraged, for example. Safety campaigns that encourage healthier attitudes toward alcohol consumption can also have an impact on sexual assault rates; this is particularly important when it comes to college campuses.

Clearly, society-level prevention takes the longest to achieve, but that doesn't mean that it is not worth pursuing. Consider, for instance, the decades of work that went into reducing tobacco smoking or the activism surrounding drinking and driving. Those campaigns are examples of two society-level interventions that took time but have improved public health over the long haul.

CENTERS FOR DISEASE CONTROL AND PREVENTION

The CDC also makes educational videos about sexual violence.

PREVENTING HARASSMENT

When it comes to sexual harassment in schools and workplaces, the public health model can also be helpful, but other prevention strategies are also necessary.

As mentioned in Chapter 1, sexual harassment is a violation of Title VII of the Civil Rights Act. As such, employers are responsible for making sure they keep their workplaces free of harassment. Here are some of the features of successful anti-harassment policies:

- Anti-harassment policies are clearly defined and explained.
- Policies are communicated to everyone who works at the company or school.
- There is follow-through to make sure people understand and observe those policies.
- Training sessions make sure people don't just hear about the rules but actually understand why they exist.
- The institution (office, school, etc.) has understandable procedures for filing harassment complaints when necessary.

KNOW THE LAW ON HARASSMENT

"Unwelcome sexual advances, requests for sexual favors, and other verbal or physical conduct of a sexual nature constitutes sexual harassment when submission to or rejection of this conduct explicitly or implicitly affects an individual's employment, unreasonably interferes with an individual's work performance or creates an intimidating, hostile, or offensive work environment."

–Definition of sexual harassment from the Equal Employment Opportunity Commission

REPORTERS REGRET REPORTING

After a spate of bad publicity relating to sexual harassment in its offices, the Fox News Network established a hotline for employees to file complaints. However, Fox employees later said that nothing ever came of the complaints that were filed. In fact, one reporter filed a lawsuit arguing that she was fired about 24 hours after using the hotline!

- Procedures have to actually be followed. It's not enough to just have a policy – the policy needs to produce some kind of investigation or results when the time comes.
- People who report problems should not be punished for speaking up. The best reporting system in the world won't be effective if people who use it are subject to **retaliation**.

IT STARTS AT THE TOP

In 2017 *Forbes* magazine outlined steps that companies should be taking to reduce sexual harassment in their offices. For the policies to be effective, *Forbes* argued, they can't **emanate** merely from the human resources department of a company, but they need to be championed by the very top, including the top boss (the chief executive officer, or CEO). Also, upper management needs to not only understand the policies, but also why they matter. As Columbia University professor Elissa Perry told a reporter, "It's not just about providing one training and you're done. It's got to be a comprehensive approach. . . . The tone is set at the top. Are they just checking a box? If they are only doing it for legal reasons, then they don't care if it works."

IT'S ALL BIG STUFF

There's an old saying about how you shouldn't "sweat the small stuff." But when it comes to harassment, there may not be such a thing as "small stuff."

Name-calling, rude jokes, "minor" unwanted touches . . . it's tempting to pass off these behaviors as insignificant. And they are, in the sense that the immediate harm caused by a naughty joke is pretty mild. The problem comes when such "small stuff" piles up over time. Lots of seemingly insignificant moments can collect together to create an environment in which sexual harassment is considered acceptable. This is true just as much in schools as it is in workplaces. When seemingly minor bullying incidents are not responded to, it's common for things to get worse. It's a bit like the "broken windows" theory" of policing, which focuses on minor offenses as a way to reduce more serious ones. When it comes to harassment, experts argue that schools and workplaces shouldn't ignore small problems and wait for something "serious" to occur.

COOL NAMES FOR WOMEN?

THE COLD FACTS: THEY'RE NOT!

This anti-harassment poster from the U.S. Defense Department's American Forces Information Service targets the idea that a minor issue, like using cute slang to refer to women, can be the beginning of a bigger problem.

WHAT IS ZERO TOLERANCE?

Zero tolerance describes the very strict enforcement of a particular set of policies. It's a term you hear a lot in educational environments. Basically it's a "no exceptions" method of applying rules. Originally, schools used zero-tolerance policies for discipline issues like drugs, weapons, or fighting in school. But more recently, harassment has also been addressed under the zero-tolerance framework. Many businesses are also instituting zero-tolerance sexual harassment policies, which can mean automatic firing for a first offense.

School administrators and corporate executives tend to like zero-tolerance policies because they take the guesswork out of punishment. No one can claim unfair treatment, because all cases are treated the same way. Also, the very term *zero tolerance* conveys the idea that administrators are serious – the very existence of the policy is seen as a **deterrent** to future incidents.

However, these policies have also come in for a lot of criticism. They've been mocked as "zero-logic" policies because they don't allow for the consideration of specific contexts. In one well-publicized 2016 case, two high school students in Escondido, California, were expelled after knives were found in their vehicles . . . because they'd been fishing, not because there was an intent to bring the knives into the school building. (After a public outcry, their expulsion was reversed.)

Critics have suggested that zero-tolerance policies

"Our tolerance is not zero, it's watch out below."

An editorial cartoon parodies the excessive nature of some zero-tolerance policies.

may actually discourage people from coming forward with problems, because they worry about the punishment being worse than the "crime." That's particularly true when it comes to harassment. It's easy to picture a situation in which a young woman receives unwanted attention from a man at work; she doesn't like it and wants it to stop; but she knows that if she goes to her boss, the man will get fired, which is not the outcome she's after at all. So instead, she says nothing, the harassment goes on, and it likely gets worse over time because no one has addressed it.

As psychologist Liane Davey told a reporter in 2017, "the problem with zero tolerance is it's very binary, [but] sexual harassment and sexual assault are not at all binary." It's true that, as noted above, even small incidents do matter. But people who study the issue have been urging both executives and school administrators to work develop more **nuanced** policies – ones that take harassment seriously but don't apply one solution to every problem.

SPEAK OUT
Against Harassment and Bullying

Unwelcome sexual advances, requests for sexual favors, and other verbal or physical conduct of a sexual nature constitute sexual harassment when this conduct explicitly or implicitly affects an individual's employment, unreasonably interferes with an individual's work performance, or creates an intimidating, hostile, or offensive work environment.

WHAT IS TITLE IX?

Earlier in the book, we mentioned Title VII of the Civil Rights Act as it relates to workplace harassment. When it comes to an educational setting, another law comes into play: Title IX of the Education Amendments Act of 1972. Title IX prohibits discrimination on the basis of gender at all schools that accept federal funding – which is most of them. For a long time, Title IX was best known as the law that forced high schools and universities to pay attention to their female athletic programs. These days, however, Title IX comes up a lot as it relates to harassment.

U.S. courts have affirmed on numerous occasions that pervasive sexual harassment constitutes a form of gender discrimination. The Supreme Court weighed in on the question in *Davis v Monroe County Board of Education* (1999). The Court found that administrators and school boards have a responsibility under Title IX to take active steps to halt sexual harassment of students. Monroe County was found to have been "deliberately indifferent" to the "severe, persistent" harassment of fifth-grader LaShonda Davis, violating her Constitutional right to an equal education.

In 2017 an Associated Press investigation uncovered 17,000 reported cases of sexual assault at K–12 schools in just 4 years (fall 2011 to spring 2015). It's worth noting that only 32 states actually track sexual assault

> "No person in the United States shall, on the basis of sex, be excluded from participation in, be denied the benefits of, or be subjected to discrimination under any education program or activity receiving Federal financial assistance."
>
> –Title IX, Educational Amendments Act of 1972

FIND OUT MORE

There is a huge amount of variance when it comes to how states track sexual violence at educational institutions. The Associated Press created an online report where you can search your state to see what their educational policies are. Point your browser to https://www.ap.org/explore/schoolhouse-sex-assault/student-sex-assault-reports-and-how-they-vary-by-state.html.

incidents. Individual school boards are allowed to decide whether and how to keep track of reports, and many opt not to do so. So even that shockingly high number is not the entire story.

Sexual harassment is often framed as a "female problem," and people tend to think of Title IX as a law designed to protect female students. But that's not the whole story. When it comes to educational settings, many young men are also victimized, and not just at the college level. In fact, the American Association of University Women released a study which found that that 87 percent of girls and 76 percent of boys experienced some form of sexual harassment between eighth and 11th grade. Title IX covers those boys, too – not just female students. And Title IX protection extends to

An installation at the University of Oregon spreads awareness about the pervasive nature of sexual assault on campuses.

LGBTQ students as well. Several lawsuits have been brought concerning the harassment of LGBTQ students and the courts found that Title IX does, indeed, offer protection to students from being singled out based on their sexual orientation or gender identity.

Administrators are expected to not only avoid harassing anyone themselves, but also to keep their eyes out for problems between students. People often think of traditional "bullying" as being separate from sexual harassment, but evidence suggests that's not true. One study found that 64 percent of students who reported being bullied were also sexually harassed. Bullying and harassment aren't always clearly distinguishable — they often go hand-in-hand.

TEXT-DEPENDENT QUESTIONS

1. What are the four parts of the social-ecological model?
2. What does the CDC's "STOP SV" acronym stand for?
3. What are some aspects of an effective anti-harassment policy?
4. What are some arguments for and against zero-tolerance policies?
5. Who does Title IX protect?

RESEARCH PROJECT

Find out about your school's policies with regard to harassment and assault. How do students go about filing complaints if they need to? What procedures are followed? Make a poster or pamphlet that explains the procedures in a way your fellow students can understand.

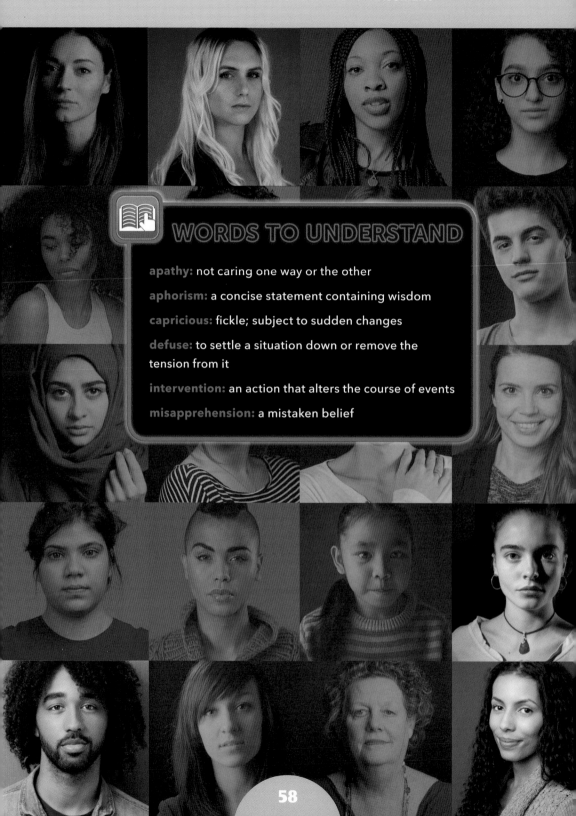

WORDS TO UNDERSTAND

apathy: not caring one way or the other

aphorism: a concise statement containing wisdom

capricious: fickle; subject to sudden changes

defuse: to settle a situation down or remove the tension from it

intervention: an action that alters the course of events

misapprehension: a mistaken belief

PREVENTION IN ACTION

In Israel in the early 1970s, the government had a discussion about how to prevent attacks on women that had been occurring in the streets late at night. Someone suggested instituting a curfew to keep women home after a certain hour. Prime Minister Golda Meir famously responded, "But it is the men who are attacking the women! If there is to be a curfew, let the men stay at home."

Meir's famous remark cuts to the heart of what can be a frustrating aspect of any discussion of prevention. On the one hand, the desire to keep vulnerable people safe is an honorable one. But on the other hand, that desire to be protective can sometimes distract from our ability to deal with the cause of the problem itself. This chapter will look at practical aspects of sexual-misconduct prevention from several different angles.

REMEMBER THIS NUMBER

National Sexual Assault Hotline 1-800-656-HOPE

WHAT IS CONSENT?

The single most important thing we can do to prevent sexual misconduct is to have a clear and thorough understanding of consent. At its simplest, consent is when one person agrees to do something (in this case, have sex) with another. But as we all know, life is complicated — when it comes to sexual consent, there is a little more to it than just agreement.

Here are the basic elements of sexual consent:

1. It's given freely. If someone has been pressured (either emotionally or physically) into saying yes, then that's not true consent.

2. It's given enthusiastically. If someone only consents to get the other person to stop pestering her or him, that, too, is not real consent.

3. It's not for everything. Consenting to one activity — let's say, kissing — does not mean you've automatically consented to another activity, such as intercourse.

4. It requires honesty. If someone consents to having sex with a condom, and then the partner removes the condom, that's not real consent either.

5. It can be revoked. Partners always have the ability to change their minds.

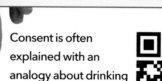

Consent is often explained with an analogy about drinking tea, as in this video.

It used to be that if someone didn't *actively resist* sexual intercourse, it was assumed that he or she was consenting. Commonly referred to as "no means no," the idea was essentially that unless someone was specifically objecting, she or he could be assumed to be consenting.

FACT CHECK!

Myth: *It's not rape unless there's fighting or resistance.*

Fact: Consent needs to be actively given. It's not enough to just say, "Well, she didn't fight me off."

These days, a form of "active consent" is required – sometimes people call it "yes means yes." Active consent requires that sexual partners say, out loud, that they are consenting to the activity. Carol Stenger, an educator at the University of Albany, uses the analogy of borrowing someone's cell phone. "You wouldn't just take it," she points out, "you'd ask for it first."

NONVERBAL CONSENT?

In 2015 a *New York Times* article on sexual consent quoted a study that found something rather troubling. According to the study, slightly over 60 percent of the men surveyed assumed that consent could be communicated through body language rather than words. The problem? In the same study, only 10 percent of women felt that they had *given* consent with body language. That suggests men may be assuming they have consent when their female partner does not think she has actually given it. The notion of body language as nonverbal consent leaves everything open to interpretation and, therefore, misunderstanding. This is why activists push for a more clear, verbal assent as the standard.

MYTHS ABOUT SEX AND RELATIONSHIPS

Even well-intentioned people can fall prey to patterns of thinking that normalize and even encourage sexual misconduct. These myths and thought patterns contribute to an environment in which sexual assault can be explained away or justified. And yet our society often passes these errors along unchallenged. Here are a few erroneous beliefs about relationships and sexuality that we can live without.

MYTH: Women turn down sex because they are "supposed to" turn it down. If you keep pushing them, they will give in because it's what they secretly want.

The aphorism that "no means no" has been repeated so often that it's become a cliché. But there's a good reason people keep saying it. It remains a common misapprehension that women are just waiting for men to come along and insist on sexual activity.

MYTH: Men are not romantic like women are; they just use romance to get sex.

This idea, that men are only motivated by their sex drives can be traced all the way back to Victorian times, and many people still believe it. But in the 1980s, sociologists Susan Sprecher and Sandra Metts created the Romantic Beliefs Scale as a way of studying romantic feelings among both women and men. They found that men score just as high (sometimes higher!) when it comes to romantic feelings for their partners. In fact, more men tend to believe in "love at first sight" than women do.

MYTH: Women have a responsibility to "take care" of men and meet their needs, be it sexually or otherwise.

Decades of feminism have made a lot of progress in correcting the belief that one gender exists to serve the other. But this belief still lingers in the subconscious of some (by no means all!) people. It comes out in a man's unwillingness to accept that a woman's preferences and needs are of equal importance to his own.

MYTH: Real men are supposed to be "players."

First, forget "supposed to" — there is no particular number of partners that anyone is supposed to have. Second, studies suggest that men don't necessarily have as many partners as they claim, while women may have more than they admit. In the late 1990s, Michael W. Wiedermann studied several surveys in which people reported the number of sex partners they'd had; ultimately he concluded that men tend to round up the total while women tend to round down. There is not as big a difference in the total number of partners for men and women, despite the bragging of certain "players."

MYTH: Women "cry rape" when they feel guilty after sex.

False claims of rape do happen. But only between 2 and 5 percent of sexual assault accusations are later found to be lies. That's equivalent to the number of times people lie about having been robbed or beaten up. So, does it happen? Yes, a small fraction of the time. But just as you'd be inclined to listen to a friend who says she got mugged, statistics say you should do the same to a friend who says she (or he!) was the victim of sexual violence.

MYTH: Women are mysterious, capricious, and basically impossible to understand.

This error feeds the assumption that women neither mean what they say nor say what they mean, and therefore there is no real point in listening to them. This denies women the right to be considered as complete people, with the same concerns, anxieties, and struggles as anyone else.

Some misconceptions about women promote the idea that they are somehow not as fully human as men are.

WHAT IS BYSTANDER TRAINING?

There are many programs designed to educate people on preventing sexual assault. One program, active since 2001, is called "No Zebras, No Excuses." The name comes from the image of a herd of zebras that stand by and watch as one of their own gets taken down by a lion. Instead of working together to chase off the lion, the zebras just watch and think, "it's not my problem," or, "I'm glad it wasn't me."

Zebras watching a lion attack one of their own is an analogy to explain a social science concept called *bystander* **apathy**. The more witnesses there are to a particular event, the less responsibility each individual feels to get involved. People think, "Well, *somebody* will do something – it's not important for me specifically to do anything." What's more, whenever a group of people witness something and no one responds, the subtext is that no one *should* respond. After all, if the situation were "that bad," then clearly somebody would step in. It's circular logic: the fact that no one steps in reinforces the idea that the event isn't bad, and the belief that the event isn't bad just encourages people to not get involved.

ASK FOR ANGELA

Hayley Child works for the local government in Lincolnshire, England. In 2016 she came up with a poster campaign to help women who were being harassed at local pubs. In numerous area pubs, the women's restrooms now have signs letting women know that if someone at the bar is making them feel unsafe, they should go to the bartender and "ask for Angela." That's a signal to the bartender they need assistance.

In 2018 the Ask for Angela campaign had gone viral, leading bars in numerous cities around the world to also adopt the practice. Other bars have their own, similar practices – such as ordering a particular drink that signals you need help.

It's On Us: Bystander Intervention Tips

1. Talk to your friends honestly and openly about sexual assault.
2. Don't be a bystander – if you see something, intervene in any way you can.
3. Trust your gut. If something looks like it might be a bad situation, it probably is.
4. Be direct. Ask someone who looks like they may need help if they're okay.
5. Get someone to help you if you see something – enlist a friend, advisor, bartender, or host to help step in.
6. Keep an eye on someone who has had too much to drink.
7. If you see someone who is too intoxicated to consent, enlist their friends to help them leave safely.
8. Recognize the potential danger of someone who talks about planning to target another person at a party.
9. Be aware if someone is deliberately trying to intoxicate, isolate, or corner someone else.
10. Get in the way by creating a distraction, drawing attention to the situation, or separating them.
11. Understand that if someone does not or cannot consent to sex, it's rape.
12. Never blame the victim.
13. If you are a victim or survivor, or helping someone in that situation, go to www.notalone.gov to get the resources and information you need. You can also call the National Sexual Assault Hotline at 1-800-656 HOPE.

Source: It's On Us, https://www.itsonus.org/wp-content/uploads/2017/04/IOU-Bystander-Intervention-Tips.pdf.

The "It's On Us" campaign was created in 2014 by the White House Task Force to Prevent Sexual Assault. A key goal is to encourage more bystander awareness in young people.

BEING A GOOD BYSTANDER

The anti-sexual violence group RAINN advises the following steps for bystanders:

- If you see an interaction between people that looks troubling or "off," try to create a distraction that may **defuse** the situation and/or allow the harassed person to get away. For instance, if you're at a party, you could interrupt an uncomfortable conversation to offer snacks or to suggest a new activity as a distraction. The specifics are not that important – the goal is to divert the focus away from the person who may be feeling uncomfortable.

- Check in with the person you're concerned about. Sometimes all you need to do is ask, "Are you okay?" You could also offer to quietly stick around so the person doesn't feel alone, saying something like, "Are you here by yourself? Would you like me to stay nearby?"

- If you feel that this is more than you can handle, ask a friend to help, too. And don't be afraid to get some sort of authority figure involved, be it an advisor, security guard, or whoever is around. We all – and teens in particular – have been taught that "snitching" is bad, but your silence may only be helping the harasser.

- As discussed earlier in the book, sexual misconduct is frequently tied up with peer pressure, especially when it comes to young people. The research tells us that when peers normalize the idea that sexual assault is okay, there will likely be more sexual assault in that peer group. So even small efforts, like speaking out when a friend makes a sexist comment, can help improve the environment as a whole.

Check out this video to learn more about bystander intervention.

"In many cases, the witness to [harassment] is more empowered than the person who is victimized. Especially if power is involved, there's a challenging dynamic for the victim to raise the issue. I strongly encourage people to stop witnessing these things and not saying anything."

—Liane Davey, psychologist

Bystander **intervention** is an approach to sexual assault prevention that emphasizes the need for people to (a) be more aware of what's going on around them, and (b) be more willing to intervene when needed. One type of intervention would be making sure that someone who has had too much to drink at a party gets home safely. Bystander awareness can also be something as simple as vocally objecting when someone makes a rape joke, or posting support for someone who is being harassed online. Bystander awareness can mean challenging the kinds of assumptions that make sexual violence more likely to occur. When "small" problems – like, say, a rape joke – go unaddressed, then larger problems become more likely.

THE ROLE OF PERSONAL RESPONSIBILITY

Let's say a female college student goes to a party. She drinks alcohol at the party, as does everyone else. She dances with a male student she likes. It gets late, and her friends have already left. The male student offers to walk her home, and she agrees. But on their way to her dormitory, they find themselves in a quiet location with no one else around, and he assaults her.

It's common for people to look at this situation and draw the following conclusions:

1. She made a bad choice by drinking alcohol.
2. She made a bad choice by staying out late.
3. She made a bad choice by agreeing to walk home with the young man.

Here's the thing, though: even if all of the above are true, none of it transfers responsibility for the assault from the perpetrator to the victim. Yes, personal responsibility is important. And *all* involved parties have personal responsibility, not just the victim.

Let's not forget: the male student in our example was also drinking. He, too, was out late. He could have offered to call her a car – instead he chose to take her to that quiet location. Perhaps our fictional "she" made a bad choice in deciding to stay out late. But surely "he" made a far *worse* choice in deciding to attack her.

Ours is a world of choices – we make them all the time. It's good to encourage people to be thoughtful about their behavior. The next page has a list of safety tips that may help you stay safe. Personal responsibility is important, and the right choice at the right time can mean the difference between a good night out and a terrible one.

But the truth is, a person can make every "safe" choice in the world and still end up being victimized. If it happens to you, it is not your fault. Even if you made some unsafe choices along the way, that does not mean you deserves blame for violent choices made by someone else.

Consenting to one sexual activity does not mean you've consented to others.

SAFETY TIPS

There is no such thing as perfect or total safety. But there are some things you can do that may help improve the level of safety in your life.

- Learn about available resources in advance. That includes both procedural things like how to report an incident, but also basic information, such as where the nurse's office and/or police station is. Find out who is available to help you *before* you need the help. Hopefully you'll never need to use resources on sexual assault, but if the issue comes up, you'll be glad you were prepared.

- Be wary about sharing personal information on social media.

- Also think twice about posting your location – are you sure you want *everyone* to know where you are at any given time? Consider turning off geolocation functions on social media sites (they are sometimes set to "on" by default, and you may not realize how much you are sharing).

- Be aware of your surroundings, especially when traveling from place to place at night. Where would you go if you suddenly found yourself in trouble? Have a Plan B for getting home in case your original route doesn't pan out.

- Make sure your cell phone is charged when you're away from home.

- Memorize a couple of key phone numbers, just in case the battery dies, and you need a ride or some other form of help.

- If you go out with someone you don't know well, make sure a friend or family member knows where you're going and who you're with.

- When meeting someone new, don't give out a lot of personal information right away. Someone you've just met doesn't need to know about your finances, where you live, whether you live alone, and so on. You don't owe an answer to every single question just because someone asks. Polite deflection is totally okay.

- If possible, attend parties with friends rather than going alone. That way you can look out for one another.

- Be careful with alcohol. The safest choice is to abstain completely, but if that's not realistic, know your limits.

- Pay attention to what you're drinking – premade punches can be risky because you have no way of knowing the ingredients. Also be aware of how many drinks you've had.

SAFETY TIPS FOR WOMEN — **SEXUAL ASSAULT PREVENTION** — ONLINE

- DON'T SHARE PERSONAL INFORMATION WITH STRANGERS

- DON'T SHARE YOUR LOCATION ONLINE

- DON'T SHARE PRIVATE PICTURES ONLINE

- FOLLOW ONLINE DATING SAFETY TIPS

- Keep an eye on your friends at parties and help them if they need it. The reverse is also true: if friends offer to help you, let them. And don't let other people give you drinks or hold them for you while you're not looking.

- If someone is making you uncomfortable, don't put that person's feelings above your own safety. It's okay to tell a little white lie to get out of a situation that feels off. You're not being silly; you're being careful.

- Trust your instincts. If you feel unsafe, listen to that feeling and do something about it.

TEXT-DEPENDENT QUESTIONS

1. Does silence automatically mean consent?
2. What is bystander intervention?
3. What are some ways bystanders can intervene safely?
4. Who is Angela?
5. What are some safety tips everyone should remember?

RESEARCH PROJECT

Find out what resources your school or community offers to support survivors of sexual violence. Gather phone numbers, websites, and other contact information and turn them into a document (poster, pamphlet, blog post, etc.) that you can share with others.

SERIES GLOSSARY OF KEY TERMS

adjudicated: when a problem is addressed in a formal setting, such as a courtroom

advocacy: championing or arguing for a particular thing

agency: the ability to take actions that affect your life or the world

allegations: claims that someone has done something wrong

amorphous: something with a vaguely defined shape

assess: evaluate

cisgender: describes a person whose gender identity matches that person's biological sex

coercion: forcing someone to do something they don't want to do

cognitive: relates to how a person thinks

complainant: legal term for someone who brings a case against another person

conflict resolution: a process through which people with disagreements can work together to solve them

consent: agreement or permission

corroborating: something that confirms a claim is true

credible: believable

demographic: relates to the different types of people in a society; age, race, and gender are examples of demographic categories

deterrent: something that discourages a particular activity

diagnosable: a health condition with specific symptoms and treatments that can be identified by a health-care professional

disordered: random; without a system

dissonance: a tension caused by two things that don't fit together

emancipated: free from certain legal or social restrictions

endemic: widespread or common among a certain group

entitlement: the sense that one has the right to something

exonerated: cleared of guilt

feign: to pretend to feel something you don't

felony: a category of serious crime; felony crimes come in several degrees, with "first degree" being the most serious, "second degree" being slightly less serious, and so on

fondling: to stroke or caress, usually with a sexual implication

idealized: describes something viewed as perfect, or better than it is in reality

incapacitated: describes the condition of being unable to respond, move, or understand

inflection point: a term borrowed from mathematics; refers to moments when there is a noticeable change (for example in public opinion)

ingratiate: to actively try to get someone to like you

internalize: to take in an idea or belief as your own

intrusive: describes something unwanted, such as "intrusive thoughts"

involuntary: a situation where you have no choice

LGBTQ: acronym for lesbian, gay, bisexual, transgender, and queer/questioning

mandatory: legally required

minor: anyone under the age of legal responsibility; usually means under 18 years old

nonconsensual: describes an act (often sexual) that one participant did not agree to

nontraditional: different from a widely accepted norm

norms: standards of what's considered typical or "normal" for a particular group or situation

nuanced: describes something that is complex; not "black and white"

nurturing: describes something that is supportive and warm

ostracized: shunned, shut out

pernicious: describes something that's very harmful but in a subtle way

pervasive: widespread

prophylactic: preventative

psychosis: mental impairment so severe the person loses connection with reality

PTSD: an acronym for post-traumatic stress disorder, a serious psychological condition caused by profoundly disturbing experiences

regressive: moving backwards, toward an earlier state of being

remorse: regret

repercussions: consequences

resilience: the ability to recover from difficulties

retaliation: revenge or punishment

self-determination: the ability to make your own decisions and follow through with them

sociopath: someone with a severe mental disorder who lacks empathy or conscience

spectrum: a range

STDs: acronym for sexually transmitted diseases

stereotype: a widely held but oversimplified or inaccurate picture of a particular type of person or group

suggestive: describes something that suggests or implies a particular idea

surveillance: observation; spying

trafficking: describes some form of illegal trade or commerce

unambiguous: very clear; not open to interpretation

FURTHER READING & INTERNET RESOURCES

BOOKS AND ARTICLES

Busch, Elizabeth Kaufer, and William E. Thro. *Title IX: The Transformation of Sex Discrimination in Education*. Critical Moments in American History. New York: Routledge, 2018.

Clarke, Annie E., and Andrea L. Pino. *We Believe You: Survivors of Campus Sexual Assault Speak Out*. New York: Holt, 2016.

Domitrz, Michael. *Can I Kiss You?: A Thought-Provoking Look at Relationships, Intimacy, and Sexual Assault*. Greenfield, WI: Awareness Publications, 2016.

Freitas, Donna. *Consent on Campus: A Manifesto*. New York: Oxford University Press, 2018.

Gay, Roxane, ed. *Not That Bad: Dispatches from Rape Culture*. New York: Harper Perennial, 2018.

Harding, Kate. *Asking For It: The Alarming Rise of Rape Culture – And What We Can Do about It*. Boston: DaCapo Press, 2015.

Lewis, Stephanie Kaplan, Annie Chandler Wang, and Windsor Hanger Western, eds. *The Her Campus Guide to College Life: How to Manage Relationships, Stay Safe and Healthy, Handle Stress, and Have the Best Years of Your Life!* New York: Simon & Schuster, 2015.

Lipman, Joanne. *That's What She Said: What Men Need to Know (and Women Need to Tell Them) About Working Together*. New York: William Morrow, 2018.

Missouri Coalition Against Domestic and Sexual Violence. "Understanding the Dynamics of Sexual Violence." March 2014. http://www.mocadsv.org//FileStream.aspx?FileID=388.

Wooten, Sara Carrigan, and Roland W. Mitchell, eds. *Preventing Sexual Violence on Campus: Challenging Traditional Approaches through Program Innovation*. New York: Routledge, 2017.

WEBSITES

CDC. "Sexual Violence: Prevention Strategies."

https://www.cdc.gov/violenceprevention/sexualviolence/prevention.html

Information about the CDC's STOP SV prevention program.

Love Is Respect.

http://www.loveisrespect.org

Packed with information about consent, abuse, harassment, and how to build safe and happy relationships. A project of the National Domestic Violence Hotline.

RAINN.

https://www.rainn.org

The Rape, Abuse, & Incest National Network is the largest anti-sexual violence program in the United States.

Safe Dates.

https://www.hazelden.org/web/public/safedates

An educational program to prevent dating violence from the Hazelden Betty Ford Foundation.

EDUCATIONAL VIDEOS

Chapter 1

This video talks about sexual harassment in the workplace.

http://x-qr.net/1KKv

Chapter 2

Check out this video from the U.S. military about assault prevention.

http://x-qr.net/1Hyo

Chapter 3

The CDC also makes educational videos about sexual violence.

http://x-qr.net/1L69

Chapter 4

Consent is often explained with an analogy about drinking tea, as in this video.

http://x-qr.net/1LLx

Check out this video to learn more about bystander intervention.

http://x-qr.net/1JFj

INDEX

AUTHOR'S BIOGRAPHY

H.W. Poole is a writer of books for young people, including *The Big World of Fun Facts* (Lonely Planet Kids) and the sets *Childhood Fears and Anxieties, Families Today,* and *Mental Illnesses and Disorders* (Mason Crest). She created the *Horrors of History* series (Charlesbridge) and the Ecosystems series (Facts On File). She was coauthor and editor of *The History of the Internet* (ABC-CLIO) which won the 2000 American Library Association RUSA award.

PHOTO CREDITS